HAJJ AND UMRAH

GUIDE WITH PICTURES

Copyright ©

Table of Contents

Chapter 1 (UMRAH)

1, Ehram

Before reaching Meeqat before Ehram: remove unwanted hair, trim nails, make ghusal (bath) and wudhu (ablution), or at least wudhu. Put on Ehram clothes.

2 white un-sewn pieces of cloth for men and regular clothes for women. Women should not cover their faces during Ehram, and men should not cover their heads during Ehram. On entering the state of hram Niyyah (intention) in any language to enter into hram or recite

اَللّٰهُمَّ إِنِّيْ أُرِيْدُ الْعُمْرَةَ فَيَسِّرْهَا لِيْ وَتَقَبَّلْهَا مِنِّيْ **"O Allah, I want to perform the Umrah, so make it easy for me and accept it from me"**	

Going to Masjid Al-Haram (Ka'bah), men recite Talbiyah loudly (women quietly).

Talbiyah Recitation:

لَبیکَ اَللّٰھُمَّ لبّیک لبَّیک لا شَرِیکَ لَکَ لَبیکَ ، اِنَّ
الحَمدَ وَ النِّعمة لَکَ وَ الملُک، لا شَرِیکَ لَکَ

(Here I am, O Allah, (in response to Your call), here I am. Here I am. You have no partner, here I am. Indeed, all the Praise, Grace and Sovereignty belong to You. You have no partner.)

Umrah (Tawaaf-ul-Qudoom) Entering Masjid Al-Haram (Sacred Mosque) in Makkah: Enter with the right foot and recite:

اَللّٰهُمَّ افْتَحْ لِيْ اَبْوَابَ رَحْمَتِكَ

(O Allah, open the doors of your mercy for me.)

- Make intention for the Tawaaf.

2, Tawaaf (Circling The Ka'bah 7 Times)

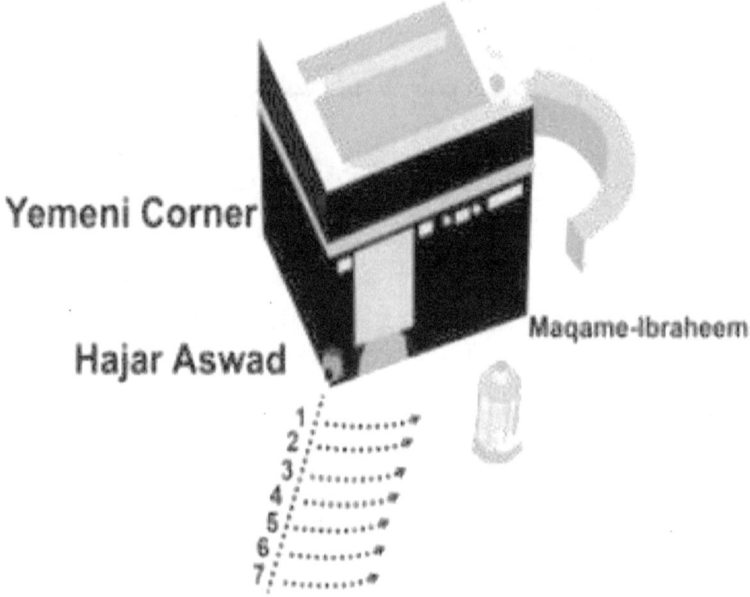

Before proceeding to the starting point of Tawaaf, Al-Hajar-ul-Aswad (the Black Stone),

1, Only men uncover the right shoulder by placing ehram underneath the right armpit (this is known as Idhtiba). When beginning each round, make a sign with your right hand towards al-Hajar-ul-Aswad (the Black Stone).

2, and recite

اَللّٰهُ اَكْبَر

(Allah is the Greatest)

Men should walk briskly (Ramal) during the first three rounds only. The remaining 4 rounds are done at a normal pace, completely around until the 7th round. No particular supplication (Dua) is essential during Tawaaf.

3. Dua (supplication) can be made during Tawaaf, except that it is Sunnah to recite the following when going between Ar-Ruknul-Yamani (Yemeni Corner):

رَبَّنَآ اٰتِنَا فِى الدُّنْيَا حَسَنَةً وَّفِى الْاٰخِرَةِ حَسَنَةً وَّقِنَا عَذَابَ النَّار

(Our Lord, give us goodness in this world and goodness in the Hereafter, and protect us from the punishment of the Fire)

Once Tawaaf is complete, cover your right shoulder and offer 2 rakaats anywhere behind the Station of Maqam-e-Ibraheem—or anywhere in the Haram. Recite Surat al-Kafirun in the first rakaat and Surat al-Ikhlas in the second rakaat.

Drink Zamzam water.

And Make Dua

3, Sa'i (Completion Of 7 Rounds Safa & Marwah)

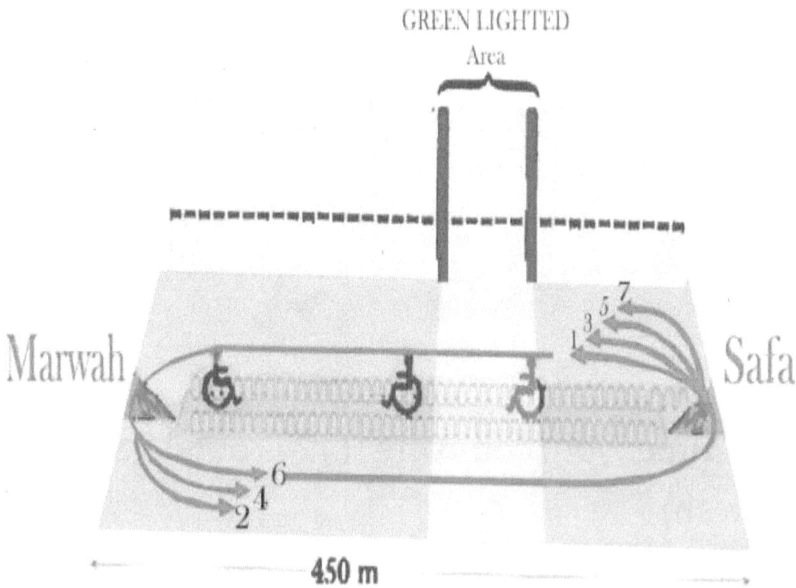

Begin Sa'i at as-Safa. Complete the walk from as-Safa to Marwah (one round), then Marwah to as-Safa (second round), and continue for seven rounds, finishing at Marwah. Upon encountering green lights, men only run from one light to another light. At the foot of As-Safa

Recite.

اِنَّ الصَّفَا وَالْمَرْوَةَ مِنْ شَعَآىِٕرِ اللّٰهِۚ فَمَنْ حَجَّ الْبَيْتَ اَوِ اعْتَمَرَ فَلَا جُنَاحَ عَلَيْهِ اَنْ يَّطَّوَّفَ بِهِمَا ۗ وَمَنْ تَطَوَّعَ خَيْرًا ۙ فَاِنَّ اللّٰهَ شَاكِرٌ عَلِيْمٌ

(Verily! As-Safa and al-Marwah are the Symbols of Allah. So it is not a sin on him who performs Hajj or 'Umrah of the House to perform the Tawa'f between them. And whoever does good voluntarily, then verily, Allah is All-Recognizer, All-Knower.)

Each time you complete one round (Safa and Marwah)

Stand on Safa and facing Qibla Recite three times.

الله أكبر- الله أكبر-الله أكبر

(Allah is the Greatest)

Then recite this dua three times.

لاإله إلا الله وحده لا شريک له، له الملک وله الحمد يحيي ويميت وهو على كل شيءٍ قدير، لا إله إلا الله وحده، أنجز وعده، ونصر عبده، وهزم الأحزاب وحده

(There is none truly worthy of worship except Allah alone, without a partner. To Him belongs all Sovereignty and all Praise. He alone gives life and causes death. He is Omnipotent over all things. There is none truly worthy of worship except Allah alone, without a partner. He has fulfilled His promise, and helped His slaves, and He alone has defeated the confederates.)

4, Shaving Head/Trimming

After completing Sa'i: men: shaving the entire head is preferable or cutting hair equally from all over the head; women: cutting one-third finger-length of hair.

Upon leaving Masjid ul-Haraam with the left foot,

Recite .

اَللّٰهُمَّ إِنِّی أَسْأَلُکَ مِنْ فَضْلِکَ

(O Allah, verily I ask You from Your Favor)

Remove Ehram, as all restrictions are now lifted.

Now Umrah Is Completed.

And if you intend to perform Hajj, then wait for the morning of 8 Dhu al-Hijjah.

Chapter 2 (HAJJ)

TYPES OF HAJJ

HAJJ. ANY PERSON INTENDING TO PERFORM HAJJ OPTS FOR EITHER ONE OF THE.

THREE TYPES OF HAJJ:

- **TAMATTU**: MAKING UMRAH, THEN HAJJ, IN THE PRESCRIBED MONTHS OF HAJJ. IT IS CONSIDERED THE BEST OF THE THREE FORMS OF HAJJ THAT THE PROPHET MUHAMMAD (PBUH) URGED HIS FOLLOWERS TO PERFORM.
- **QIRAAN** : MAKING UMRAH AND HAJJ AT THE SAME TIME.
- **IFRAAD**: MAKING HAJJ ONLY; WITHOUT UMRAH.

IF YOU SELECT TAMATTU OR QIRAAN, YOU MUST PERFORM THE UDHIYA (SACRIFICE) (QURBANI IN URDU).

HAJJ journey

- **Upon arrival in Makkah.** Make Tawaaf.
- **8th Dhul-Hijjah.** Wearing The ehram , Stay In Mina.
- **9th Dhul-Hijjah.** Stay In Arafah, Stay In Muzdalifah.
- **10th Dhul-Hijjah.** Stoning The Pillars, Performing The Udhiya (Sacrifice) , Shave Head, Tawaaful-Ifaadhah.
- **Upon departure from Makkah.** Tawaaful-Widaa.

8th Day Of Dhul-Hijjah (Yawmut-Tarwiyah)

Enter state of ehram.

Make intent for Hajj, reciting

اللهم إني أريد الحج فيسره لي وتقبله مني Oh Allah, I want Hajj, so make it easy for me and accept it from me.	

Standing, face the Qiblah recite the Talbiyah:

لَبیکَ اَللّٰهُمَّ لبّیک لبَّیک لا شَرِیکَ لَکَ لَبیکَ ، اِنَّ

الحَمدَ وَ النِّعمة لَکَ وَ المُلکَ، لا شَرِیکَ لَکَ

(Here I am, O Allah, (in response to Your call), here I am. Here I am. You have no partner, here I am. Indeed, all the Praise, Grace and Sovereignty belong to You. You have no partner.)

- Between the time period after Fajar and before Duhur goes to Mina (preferably in the morning),

Stay in Mina

Pray Dhuhr, 'Asr, Maghrib, and 'Isha at Mina. Engage in Ibadah (worship) all day.

9th Day Of Dhul-Hijjah (Yawmu 'Arafah)

Stay in 'Arafah

- Pray Fajr in Mina.
- Go to Arafat any time after sunrise. Stopover if possible at Namirah 7 (a place close to 'Arafah; there is now a Masjid there) and remain there until after Zawaal

(sun at highest point; no shadow) and listen to the Khutbah. If this is not possible, it is permissible to proceed to 'Arafah, remaining there until sunset. Stand upon the rocks at the bottom of the Mount of Mercy (Jabalur-Rahmah); if not, then all of 'Arafah is a standing place. Facing the Qiblah with raised hands, supplicate and also recite the Talbiyah. It is encouraged to frequently recite the following:

لاإله إلا الله وحده لا شريک له، له الملک وله

الحمد يحيي ويميت وهو على كل شيءٍ قدير

(There is none truly worthy of worship except Allah alone, without a partner. To Him belongs all Sovereignty and all Praise. He alone gives life and causes death. He is Omnipotent over all things.)

this is the best supplication to recite on this great day.

- Pray Dhuhr & Asr at Arafah.

- Perform WUQOF (stand and pray), make dua (supplications), and seek forgiveness until sunset.
- After sunset go to Muzdalifah.

Stay In Muzdalifah

- Pray Maghrib & Isha together at Muzdalifah.
- In Muzdalifah or Mina, collect 70 pebbles for stoning.
- Spend the night in Ibadah (worship) or go to sleep until Fajr.

10th Day Of Dhul-Hijjah (Yawmun-Nahr)

- Pray Fajr in Muzdalifah.
- Leave for Mina after Fajr. Between the time periods of after sunrise until night, calmly proceed to Jamaratul-'Aqabah al-Kubraa for stoning. Facing Jamarah, with Makkah to your left and Mina to your right, throw seven stones at Jamarah reciting

الله أكبر

Allah is the Greatest (after each throw).

- Performing the Hdhiya (sacrifice), If a sacrificial ticket has been purchased, this is a permissible alternative; otherwise, calmly proceed to a slaughterhouse in Mina for sacrifice.

- Shave/Trim Hair.

  After the sacrifice, men: shaving the head is preferable, or cut hair equally from all over the head; women: cutting one-third finger length of hair.

- Remove ehram, as all restrictions are now lifted. Go to Makkah to perform Tawaaful-Ifaadhah.

Tawaaful-Ifaadhah

- Go to Makkah and perform Tawaaful-Ifaadhah. It can be performed anytime up to the sunset of the 12th Dhul Hijjah. Upon entering Masjid ul-Haraam with the right foot, recite Dua entering Masjid. (See the Umrah section in Chapter 1). No ehram is required. Start at al-Hajarul-Aswad (Black Stone).
- Once Tawaaf is complete, offer 2 rakaats anywhere behind the Station of Maqam-e-Ibraheem or anywhere in the Haram: Recite Surat al-Kafirun in the 1st raka'a and Surat al-Ikhlas in the 2nd raka'a.

- Drink Zamzamwater – Make Du'aa
- Perform Sa'i (See Umrah section Chapter 1)
- Upon the completion of the Sa'i, all restrictions are now lifted.
- Return to Mina. Upon leaving al-Masjid ul-Haraam with the left foot, recite the dua of leaving the Masjid (see Umrah section, Chapter 1).

11th Dhul-Hijja

Stay In Mina For Stoning

From the time period after Zawaal (sun at highest point—no shadow) until the night, stone all three Jamarats, 21 required per day. Facing first Jamarah (smallest), with Makkah to your left and Mina to your right, throw each of the seven stones at Jamarah reciting

الله أكبر

Allah is the Greatest (after each throw).

After stoning the first Jamarah, face Qiblah (with the first Jamarah to your right), raise your hands, and supplicate as you wish. Then, calmly proceed to the second (middle) Jamarah. Facing the second Jamarah, with Makkah to your left and Mina to your right, throw each of the seven stones at Jamarah, reciting

الله أكبر

Allah is the Greatest (after each throw).

After stoning the second Jamarah, face Qiblah (with the second Jamarah to your right), raise your hands, and supplicate as you wish. Then, calmly proceed to the third jamarah (Al-'Aqabah al-Kubraa). Facing the third Jamarah, with Makkah to your left and Mina to your right, throw each of the seven stones at Jamarah, reciting

الله أكبر

Allah is the Greatest (after each throw).

After stoning the final Jamarah, move onwards without supplicating.

12th Dhul-Hijjah

- If Tawaaf Ifaadhah 8 has still not been performed, go to Makkah and perform Tawaf. Pray two rakaats, drink from Zam Zam, and perform Sa'ee. Return back to Mina.
- From the time period between after Zawaal (after midday) until night, stone all 3 Jamarat with 7 pebbles for each one. Leave Mina for Makkah before sunset, if possible. If you can't leave, stay at Mina.

13 th Dhul-Hijja

- If you didn't leave Mina, beginning after Fajr, stone all 3 Jamarat with 7 pebbles for each Jamarat.
- Leave for Makkah.
- Before your final departure from Makkah, perform Tawaaf-ul-Wadaa' (Farewell Tawaf) as your last act.

Hajj and Umrah have been completed.

Notes

If possible, cling to the area between the corner of Hajarul-Aswad (the Black Stone) and the door.

If possible, touch the Black Stone with the right hand and also kiss it; if not, simply make a sign towards it with the right hand.

If possible, touch Ruknul-Yamani (Yemeni Corner) each time; this is best; if not, then do not make any sign towards it.

A place close to 'Arafah—there is now a mosque there. If this is not possible, it is permissible to proceed to 'Arafah.

Tawaaful-Ifaadhah (Tawaaf ul Ziyarrat in Urdu) can be performed on the 10th. Women should allow extra days for Tawaaf in Makkah in case of menses.8. ston They are all the same size. You can also pick up the pebbles in Mina. You will need only 7 pebbles on the 10th and 42 afterwards (49 total). You will need 21 extra pebbles if you are staying for the 13th of Dhul-Hijjah (70 total). They must not be bigger than a chickpea. (Approximately 1cm across = 0.39 inches.).

It is permissible to perform Tawaaf-ul-Wadaa' on the 12th day of DhulHijjah (as long as you leave Mina before sunset), thus missing the recommended (but not compulsory) day of stoning.

Here it will be appropriate to write the Masnoon Dua's of Hajj and Umrah.

MASNOON DUA'S OF HAJJ AND UMRAH

TALBIYAH OF HAJJ

لَبَّيْكَ، اَللّٰهُمَّ لَبَّيْكَ، لَبَّيْكَ لَا شَرِيْكَ لَكَ لَبَّيْكَ، إِنَّ الْحَمْدَ وَالنِّعْمَةَ لَكَ وَالْمُلْكَ، لَا شَرِيْكَ لَكَ
I am here, O Allah! I am present, You have no partner, I am present, praise and blessing belong to You alone, and the king also, You have no partner.

SPECIAL DUA DAY OF ARAFAH

لَا إِلٰهَ إِلَّا اللهُ وَحْدَهُ لَا شَرِيْكَ لَهُ، لَهُ الْمُلْكُ وَلَهُ الْحَمْدُ وَهُوَ عَلٰى كُلِّ شَيْءٍ قَدِيْرٌ
There is no god but Allah; He is the One God; He has no partner; He is subject to Him; He alone is worthy of praise; and everything is under His power.

SECOND DUA DAY OF ARAFAH

اَللّٰهُمَّ إِنَّكَ تَسْمَعُ كَلَامِيْ وَتَرٰى مَكَانِيْ وَتَعْلَمُ سِرِّيْ وَعَلَانِيَتِيْ لَا يَخْفٰى عَلَيْكَ شَيْءٌ مِّنْ أَمْرِيْ وَأَنَا الْبَائِسُ الْفَقِيْرُ الْمُسْتَغِيْثُ الْمُسْتَجِيْرُ الْوَجِلُ الْمُشْفِقُ الْمُقِرُّ الْمُعْتَرِفُ بِذَنْبِهٖ، أَسْأَلُكَ مَسْأَلَةَ الْمِسْكِيْنِ وَأَبْتَهِلُ إِلَيْكَ ابْتِهَالَ الْمُذْنِبِ الذَّلِيْلِ

<table>
<tr><td>وَأَدْعُوكَ دُعَاءَ الْخَائِفِ الضَّرِيرِ وَدُعَاءَ مَنْ خَضَعَتْ لَكَ رَقَبَتُهُ وَفَاضَتْ لَكَ عَبْرَتُهُ وَذَلَّ جَسَدُهُ وَرَغِمَ لَكَ أَنْفُهُ اَللّٰهُمَّ لَا تَجْعَلْنِي بِدُعَائِكَ شَقِيًّا وَّكُنْ بِي رَؤُوفًا رَّحِيمًا يَّا خَيْرَ الْمَسْئُولِينَ وَيَا خَيْرَ الْمُعْطِينَ</td></tr>
<tr><td>O Allah! He listens to me and sees the situation I am in, and he is aware of my inner and outer appearance. Nothing I say is hidden from you. I am miserable, I am in need, I am crying, I am sheltered, I am longing, I am harassed, and I am confessing my sins. I ask you as a humble poor person asks. I growl before you like a sinner growls humiliated. And I pray to you as a fearful disaster prays. And I ask like a servant whose neck is bowed before you and tears are flowing, who is humbled before you with his body, and who is rubbing his nose before you. O Allah! So don't make me unable to make this supplication, and be kind and merciful to me. O the best of those who ask and give to those who ask.</td></tr>
</table>

DUA AT THE TIME OF ISTILAM THE BLACK STONE

<table>
<tr><td>بِسْمِ اللهِ وَاللهُ أَكْبَرُ اَللّٰهُمَّ إِيْمَانًا بِكَ وَتَصْدِيقًا بِكِتَابِكَ وَوَفَاءً بِعَهْدِكَ وَاتِّبَاعًا لِّسُنَّةِ نَبِيِّكَ صَلَّى اللهُ عَلَيْهِ وَسَلَّمَ</td></tr>
<tr><td>I start with the name of Allah and Allah is the greatest, O Allah! Believing in You, confirming Your Book and</td></tr>
</table>

following the Sunnah of Your Prophet (peace be upon him).

DUA WHEN LOOKING AT KAABA SHARIF

When looking at the Ka'ba Sharif, recite the takbeer and recite this

اَللّٰهُمَّ أَنْتَ السَّلَامُ وَمِنْكَ السَّلَامُ فَحَيِّنَا رَبَّنَا بِالسَّلَامِ اَللّٰهُمَّ زِدْ هٰذَا الْبَيْتَ
تَشْرِيْفًا وَّتَعْظِيْمًا وَّمَهَابَةً وَّزِدْ مَنْ حَجَّهٗ أَوِ اعْتَمَرَهٗ تَكْرِيْمًا وَّتَشْرِيْفًا وَّتَعْظِيْمًا
وَّبِرًّا

O Allah! You are the one who will be safe, and only you can get safety, so keep us alive, our Lord! With security. O Allah! Increase the dignity, honor, respect, goodness, and awe of this house of yours, and increase the greatness, nobility, goodness, and awe of whoever visits it, whether he is a Hajj or Umrah pilgrim.

DUA BETWEEN RUKAN YAMANI AND HAJAR ASWAD

رَبَّنَا اٰتِنَا فِي الدُّنْيَا حَسَنَةً وَّفِي الْاٰخِرَةِ حَسَنَةً وَّقِنَا عَذَابَ النَّارِ

O our Lord! Grant us the blessings of this world and the hereafter and save us from the punishment of Hellfire.

SECOND DUA BETWEEN RUKAN YAMANI AND HAJAR ASWAD

اَللّٰهُمَّ إِنِّيْ أَسْأَلُكَ الْعَفْوَ وَالْعَافِيَةَ فِي الدُّنْيَا وَالْاٰخِرَةِ رَبَّنَا اٰتِنَا فِي الدُّنْيَا حَسَنَةً وَّفِي الْاٰخِرَةِ حَسَنَةً وَّقِنَا عَذَابَ النَّارِ
O Allah! I ask you for forgiveness and peace in this world and the hereafter, O our Lord! Grant us the blessings of this world and the hereafter and save us from the punishment of Hellfire.

DUA RECITED DURING TAWAAF

سُبْحَانَ اللهِ وَالْحَمْدُ لِلّٰهِ وَلَا إِلٰهَ إِلَّا اللهُ وَاللهُ أَكْبَرُ وَلَا حَوْلَ وَلَا قُوَّةَ إِلَّا بِاللهِ
Glorified is the Self of Allah and all praise is due to Him and there is none worthy of worship except Allah, and there is no power and strength except with the help of Allah.

It was narrated from Hazrat Abu Huraira (RA) that the Prophet (PBUH) said, "Whoever circumambulates the House of Allah and does not talk but keeps reciting the above-mentioned words, ten sins are forgiven and ten good deeds are recorded. Ten levels rise.

THE THIRD DUA BETWEEN RUKAN YAMANI AND HAJAR ASWAD

رَبِّ قَنِّعْنِيْ بِمَا رَزَقْتَنِيْ وَبَارِكْ لِيْ فِيْهِ وَاخْلُفْ عَلٰى كُلِّ غَائِبَةٍ لِّيْ بِخَيْرٍ

O Lord! Grant me contentment with the sustenance that has been given and grant me blessings in it and watch over my occultation with goodness.

DUA TO BE RECITED WHILE DOING RAMAL

اَللّٰهُمَّ اجْعَلْهُ حَجًّا مَّبْرُوْرًا وَّذَنْبًا مَّغْفُوْرًا وَّسَعْيًا مَّشْكُوْرًا
O Allah! Accept Hajj and forgive sins and give the best reward for hard work.

DUA OF THROW STONES TO JAMARAT

Recite this after the Rami of Jamarat Uqbah (Allah Akbar while throwing pebbles).

اَللّٰهُمَّ اجْعَلْهُ حَجًّا مَّبْرُوْرًا وَّذَنْبًا مَّغْفُوْرًا
O Allah! Accept Hajj and forgive sins.

DUA RECITED IN THE LAST FOUR CYCLES OF TAWAAF

اَللّٰهُمَّ اغْفِرْ وَارْحَمْ وَاعْفُ عَمَّا تَعْلَمُ وَأَنْتَ الْأَعَزُّ الْأَكْرَمُ اَللّٰهُمَّ اٰتِنَا فِي الدُّنْيَا حَسَنَةً وَّفِي الْاٰخِرَةِ حَسَنَةً وَّقِنَا عَذَابَ النَّارِ
O Allah! Forgive us, have mercy on us and forgive us

those who know our sins, You are the Honorable and the Merciful, O Allah! Grant us the blessings of this world and the hereafter, and save us from the punishment of hellfire.

DUA RECITED NEAR SAFA HILL

إِنَّ الصَّفَا وَالْمَرْوَةَ مِنْ شَعَائِرِ اللهِ اَبْدَءُ بِمَا بَدَأَ اللهُ بِهٖ

Safa and Marwah are among the main signs of Allah, I begin as Allah began.

DUA RECITED ON SAFA HILL

When starting Sa'i, when you climb the hill of Safa, look towards Baitullah Sharif and recite Takbeer and Tahleel and recite this dua.

لَا إِلٰهَ إِلَّا اللهُ وَحْدَهٗ لَا شَرِيْكَ لَهٗ لَهُ الْمُلْكُ وَلَهُ الْحَمْدُ يُحْيِيْ وَيُمِيْتُ وَهُوَ عَلٰى كُلِّ
شَيْءٍ قَدِيْرٌ. لَا إِلٰهَ إِلَّا اللهُ أَنْجَزَ وَعْدَهٗ وَنَصَرَ عَبْدَهٗ وَهَزَمَ الْأَحْزَابَ وَحْدَهٗ

There is no god but Allah, He is One, He has no partner, to Him is all praise, He is Able to do all things, there is no god but Allah, He fulfills His promise and helps His servant. And alone defeated the army of the infidels.

DUA RECITED NEAR MARWAH HILL

إِنَّ الصَّفَا وَالْمَرْوَةَ مِنْ شَعَائِرِ اللّٰهِ
Safa and Marwah are among the main signs of Allah.

DUA RECITED ON MARWAH HILL

When starting Sa'i, when you climb the hill of Marwah, look towards Baitullah Sharif and recite Takbeer and Tahleel and recite this dua.

لَا إِلٰهَ إِلَّا اللّٰهُ وَحْدَهُ لَا شَرِيْكَ لَهُ لَهُ الْمُلْكُ وَلَهُ الْحَمْدُ يُحْيِي وَيُمِيْتُ وَهُوَ عَلٰى كُلِّ شَيْءٍ قَدِيْرٌ. لَا إِلٰهَ إِلَّا اللّٰهُ أَنْجَزَ وَعْدَهُ وَنَصَرَ عَبْدَهُ وَهَزَمَ الْأَحْزَابَ وَحْدَهُ
There is no god but Allah, He is One, He has no partner, to Him is all praise, He is Able to do all things, there is no god but Allah, He fulfills His promise and helps His servant. And alone defeated the army of the infidels.

DUA IN JANNAT AL-BAQI

اَلسَّلَامُ عَلَيْكُمْ دَارَ قَوْمٍ مُّؤْمِنِيْنَ وَأَتَاكُمْ مَّا تُوْعَدُوْنَ غَدًا مُّؤَجَّلُوْنَ وَإِنَّا إِنْ شَاءَ اللّٰهُ بِكُمْ لَاحِقُوْنَ اَللّٰهُمَّ اغْفِرْ لِأَهْلِ بَقِيْعِ الْغَرْقَدِ
Peace be upon you, O family of believers! He who was promised to you yesterday came to you, whose time

was fixed, and God willing, we are also going to meet you, O Allah! Forgive the people of Al-Baqi.

ANOTHER DUA RECITED ON SAFA HILL

اَللّٰهُمَّ أَحْيِنِيْ عَلٰى سُنَّةِ نَبِيِّكَ صَلَّى اللهُ عَلَيْهِ وَسَلَّمَ وَتَوَفَّنِيْ عَلٰى مِلَّتِهٖ وَأَعِذْنِيْ مِنْ مُّضِلَّاتِ الْفِتَنِ

O Allah! Keep me alive on the Sunnah of your Prophet ﷺ and give me death on the way of the Holy Prophet ﷺ and grant me refuge from misguided temptations.

DUA RECITED DURING SA'I

رَبِّ اغْفِرْ وَارْحَمْ إِنَّكَ أَنْتَ الْأَعَزُّ الْأَكْرَمُ

O Lord! Forgive me and have mercy on me. You are the Most Honorable and the Most Merciful.

THIRD DUA DAY OF ARAFAH

Read this after Asr in Maqam Arafah

اَللّٰهُ أَكْبَرُ وَلِلّٰهِ الْحَمْدُ اَللّٰهُ أَكْبَرُ وَلِلّٰهِ الْحَمْدُ لَا إِلٰهَ إِلَّا اللهُ وَحْدَهٗ لَهُ الْمُلْكُ وَلَهُ الْحَمْدُ اَللّٰهُمَّ اهْدِنِيْ بِالْهُدٰى وَوَفِّقْنِيْ بِالتَّقْوٰى وَاغْفِرْ لِيْ فِي الْآخِرَةِ وَالْأُوْلٰى

Allah is the Greatest and to Allah is all praise, there is no god but Allah, He is One, to Him is the Kingdom, and to Him is all praise, O Allah! Guide me to the straight path, and grant me Taqwa, and forgive me in this world and the Hereafter.

DUA OFFERED TO THE SACRIFICER

When someone offers a sacrifice of his family and wealth, then pray for him like this

بَارَكَ اللهُ لَكَ فِيْ أَهْلِكَ وَمَالِكَ
May Allah bless and your family and your wealth.

Visiting Madina - Masjid-Al-Nabawi – Masjid Quba.

Visiting Madina is not an obligatory act for either Hajj or Umrah, but there is great value in visiting Masjid-e-Nabawi (the Prophet's Mosque).

The Prophet (sallallahu alayhi wa sallam) has said :

"One prayer in this mosque (Madina) of mine is better than 1,000 prayers offered anywhere else except the Masjid Al-Haram (Makkah), and one prayer in Masjid AlHaram is better than 100,000 prayers in any other mosque."

He (SAW) also said: "Whoever makes ablutions at home and then goes and prays in Masjid Quba (the first mosque built in Islam), will have a reward like that of an Umrah."

سُبْحَانَكَ اللَّهُمَّ وَبِحَمْدِكَ أَشْهَدُ أَن لَّا إِلَهَ إِلَّا أَنْتَ اسْتَغْفِرُكَ وَأَتُوبُ إِلَيْكَ

ABOUT THE AUTHOR

Ibn-e-Anees is an accomplished Islamic scholar, holding a master's degree from Wifaq-ul-Madaris Al-Arabiya. Residing in Karachi, his profound expertise in Islamic education imbues his insightful writing with a deep understanding of the subject matter.

Many-Thanks!

Dear Esteemed Reader,

I want to express my sincere gratitude for choosing to read my book. Your decision to explore the pages I've written means a lot to me, and I truly hope the words within have brought you enjoyment, inspiration, or a new perspective.

Your feedback is incredibly important to me, and I look forward to hearing about your experience with the book. Thank you once again for being a part of this literary journey with me.

Warm regards.

Ibn-e-Anees

بداية الصفا
SAFA START
شروع صفا

QAID
SAMAYA GROUP

Did you love Journey of a Lifetime: A Comprehensive Guide to Hajj and Umrah with Stunning Visuals? Then you should read Halal Technique of Sacrifice (Qurbani) and Dua: A Comprehensive Guide for Eid al-Adha Rituals by ibn-eAnees!

"Halal Technique of Sacrifice (Qurbani) and Dua" is a comprehensive guidebook that offers a profound exploration of the Islamic tradition of Qurbani, the ritualistic sacrifice carried out during the Eid al-Adha festival. Authored with a deep understanding of Islamic teachings and practices, this book provides stepby-step instructions on performing the Qurbani in a halal (permissible) manner, adhering to the principles outlined in the Quran and Sunnah. Within its pages, readers will find a meticulous breakdown of the entire process, from selecting the appropriate animal to the actual act of sacrifice, ensuring that each step is carried out with utmost reverence and adherence to Islamic principles. The book elucidates the importance of fulfilling this sacred obligation

1. https://books2read.com/u/mqNaO1

2. https://books2read.com/u/mqNaO1

and elucidates the wisdom behind the ritual, allowing readers to gain a deeper understanding of the spiritual significance and purpose of Qurbani. Moreover, "Halal Technique of Sacrifice (Qurbani) and Dua" includes a comprehensive collection of supplications (dua) that can be recited before, during, and after the Qurbani, providing a valuable resource for individuals seeking to enhance their spiritual connection and engage in meaningful prayers during this auspicious occasion. These dua are carefully selected from authentic sources and serve as a guide to seek blessings, express gratitude, and invoke divine mercy. Whether one is a novice seeking to understand the intricate details of the Qurbani ritual or a seasoned practitioner wishing to deepen their knowledge, this book serves as a trusted companion, offering a wealth of information, practical guidance, and spiritual insights. "Halal Technique of Sacrifice (Qurbani) and Dua" aims to empower readers with the knowledge and understanding necessary to perform this sacred act in accordance with Islamic principles, fostering a deeper connection to Allah and enriching the spiritual experience of Eid al-Adha.

Also by ibn-e-Anees

- Halal Technique of Sacrifice (Qurbani) and Dua: A Comprehensive Guide for Eid al-Adha Rituals
- Journey of a Lifetime: A Comprehensive Guide to Hajj and Umrah with Stunning Visuals
- 40 Rabbana Duas
- First Murder on Earth: Life of Prophet Adam (AS)
- 99 Names of Allah and Attributes of the Divine
- King of Wisdom: The Enchanting Tale of Prophet Sulaiman (PBUH)
- Easy Islam Birth to Death
- First Ship on Earth

والحمد لله رب العٰلمين وصلّى الله على خير خلقه محمد وأصحابه اجمعين

www.ingramcontent.com/pod-product-compliance
Lightning Source LLC
LaVergne TN
LVHW090430210926
848480LV00002B/772